# *STRAUSS WAI*
# *for Easy Piano*

## CONTENTS

Arranged and edited by Mark Phillips

ISBN: 978-0-9850501-3-9

A. J. Cornell Publications

# The Artist's Life

by Johann Strauss

**Waltz tempo**

# The Blue Danube

by Johann Strauss

**Waltz tempo**

**Fine**

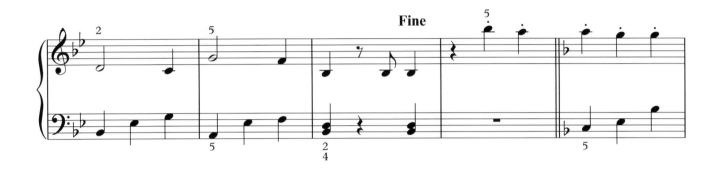

*D.C. al Fine*

# Cagliostro Waltz

by Johann Strauss

**Waltz tempo**

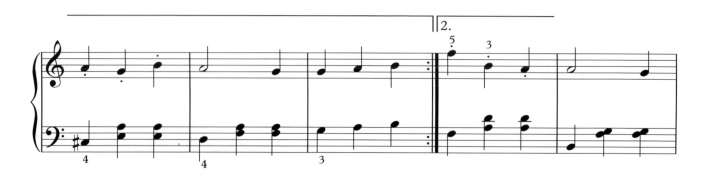

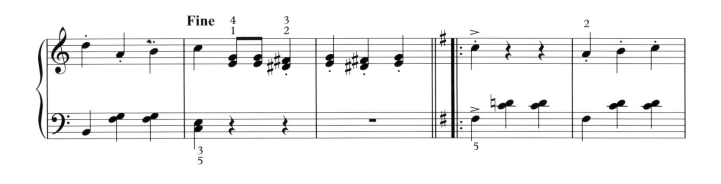

*D.S. al Fine*
*(take 2nd ending)*

7

# Emperor Waltz

by Johann Strauss

**Waltz tempo**

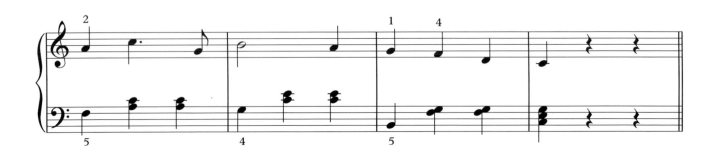

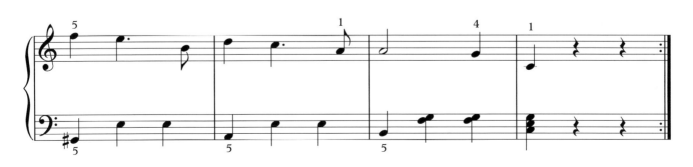

# Kiss Waltz

by Johann Strauss

**Waltz tempo**

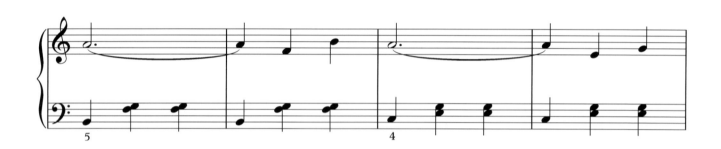

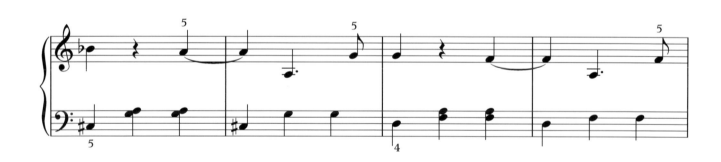

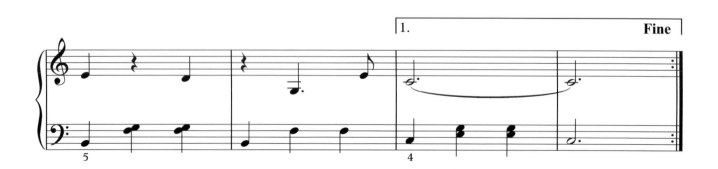

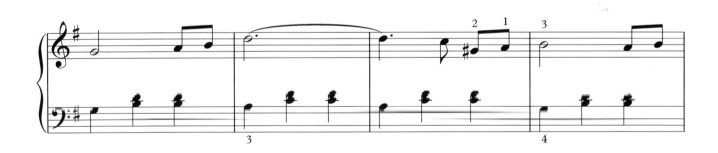

**D.C. al Fine**
*(take 1st ending)*

11

# Roses from the South

by Johann Strauss

**Waltz tempo**

14

# Tales from the Vienna Woods

by Johann Strauss

15

16

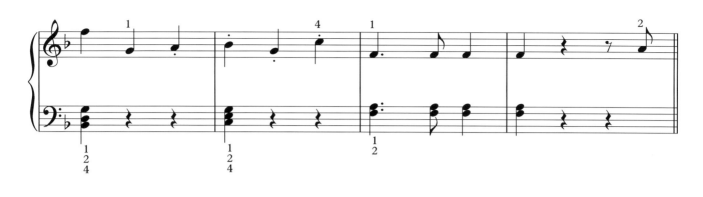

# A Thousand and One Nights

by Johann Strauss

**Waltz tempo**

18

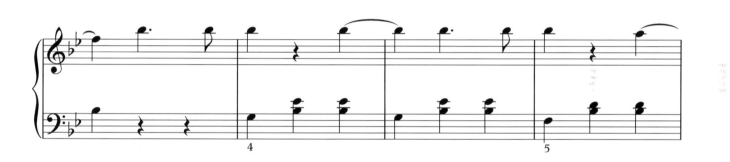

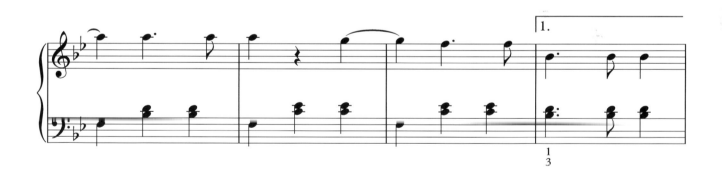

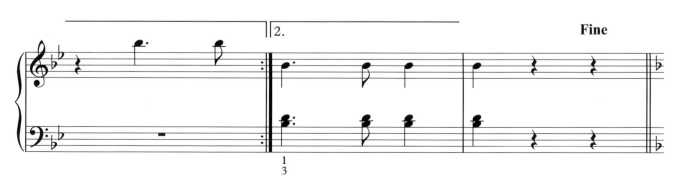

*D.C. al Fine*
*(take 2nd ending)*

# Treasure Waltz

by Johann Strauss

21

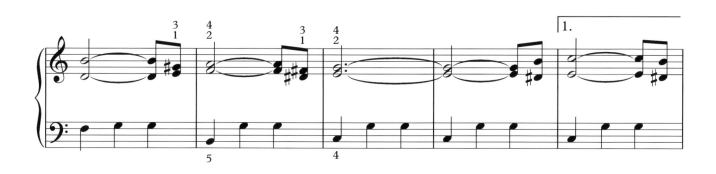

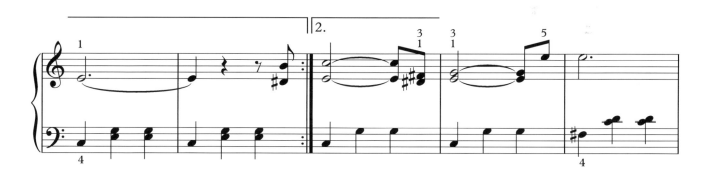
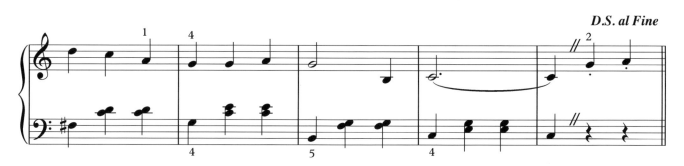

# Vienna Life

by Johann Strauss

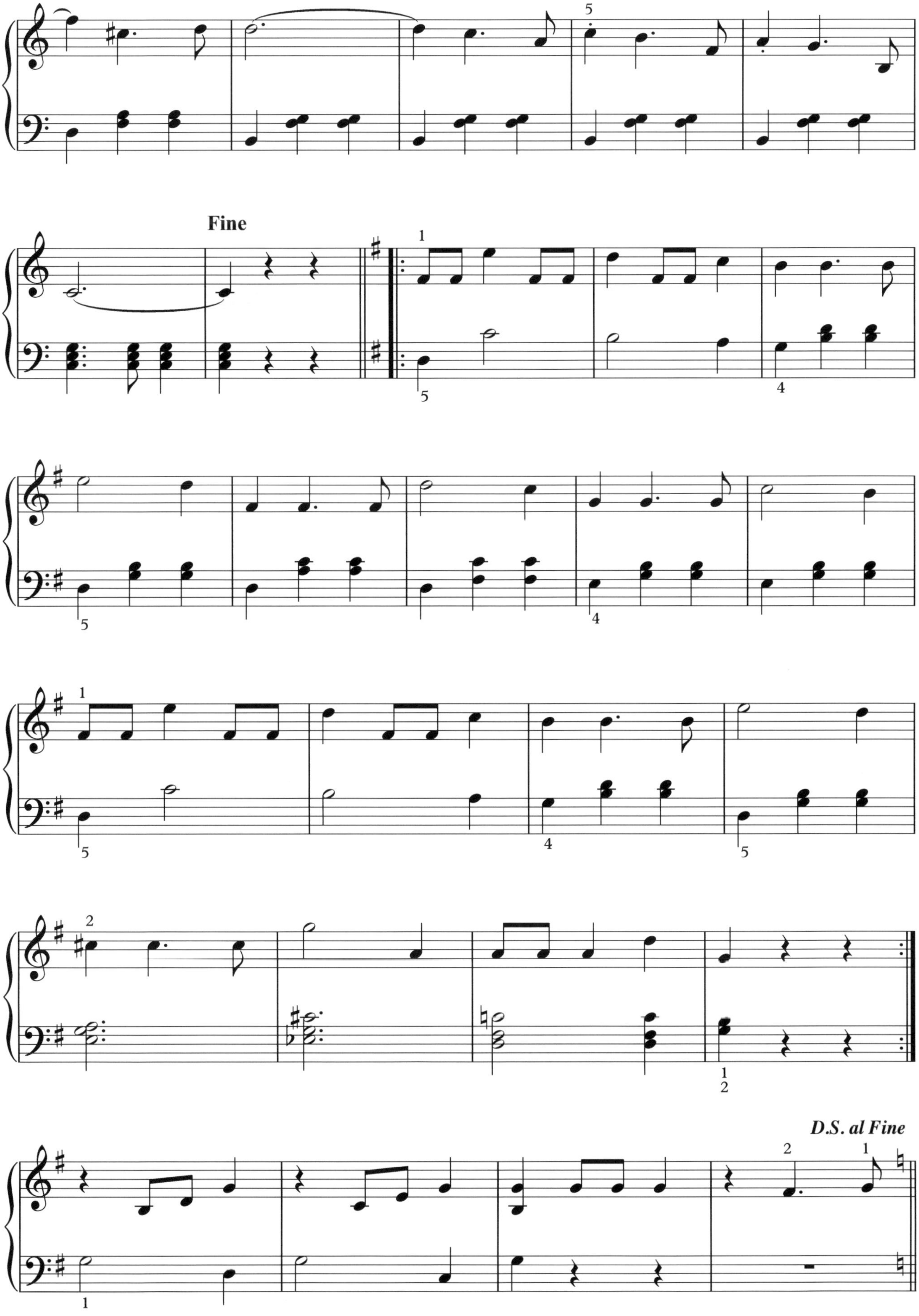
Fine
D.S. al Fine

# Where the Lemon Trees Bloom

by Johann Strauss

**Waltz tempo**

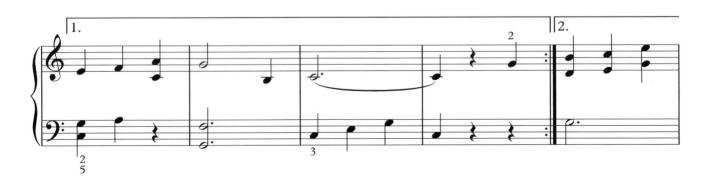

26

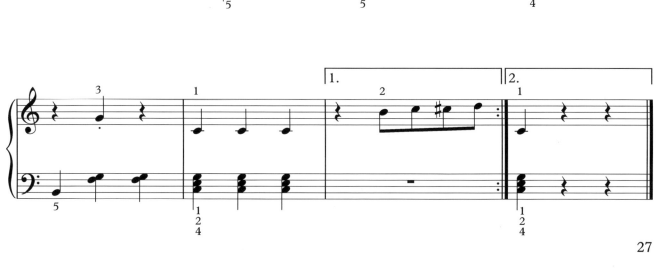

27

# Wine, Women and Song

by Johann Strauss

**Waltz tempo**

# ABOUT THE COMPOSER

Johann Strauss, Jr. (1825–1899) was born in Vienna, Austria. His father, Johann Strauss, was a well-known composer, the first to elevate dance music, especially the waltz, to an artistic plane, but he was bitterly opposed to his son's becoming a musician. The boy's mother, however, paid for his instruction on the violin. When Johann was nineteen years of age he left home to conduct a restaurant orchestra at Hietzing, Austria. There he began to present his own compositions, mainly waltzes, and the restaurant soon became crowded with admiring listeners. In 1849, after his father's death, he united his own orchestra with that of his father and began a series of tours of Europe. Everywhere he appeared he received great praise for the grace and beauty of his original dance music. In 1855 he became conductor of summer concerts in Saint Petersburg and from 1863 to 1870 was conductor of the Russian Court balls. His last days were spent at Vienna, where he died on June 3, 1899. His five hundred dance compositions have won him the title of the Waltz King. He also composed several successful operettas, among them *Indigo, A Night in Venice,* and *Prince Methusalem.*

Made in the USA
Las Vegas, NV
24 February 2024

86241101R00020